LITTL

In Inca Times

Anita Ganeri

Kingfisher

Contents

A mountain people

About seven hundred years ago, a small group of people called the Incas lived in the Andes mountains of South America. For two hundred years the Incas fought with and conquered their neighbours, until they had created a great empire.

In 1532, Spanish soldiers arrived in the empire. They were amazed at all the Incas' wealth, and wanted to win it for themselves. In just a few months, the Inca empire was defeated.

A huge empire

The Inca empire stretched for more than 3,000 kilometres along the Pacific coast. Many of its towns, such as Machu Picchu (below), were built high up in the Andes mountains. Ruins of Machu Picchu's buildings can still be seen in Peru today.

River Amazon

Amazon rainforest

Machu Picchu

Cuzco

Lake Titicaca

Andes mountains

Pacific Ocean

Inca Empire

Ruling the empire

The leader of the Incas was the Sapa Inca – the 'only emperor'. The Incas believed that he was descended from the Sun god. The Sapa Inca ruled very strictly, with the help of his noblemen. Everyone had to pay a tax to the emperor, in the form of food, clothing or other goods.

The Inca emperor wore fine clothes decorated with colourful patterns, and heavy, golden jewellery.

RELAY RUNNERS

The emperor used relay runners to carry messages or packages all over the empire. Each runner blew on a conch shell to warn the next runner that he was coming. In this way, a parcel could be carried over 240 kilometres in one day.

The wife of the emperor was called the Coya. She had an important part to play in ruling the empire, and often took the emperor's place if he was away on business.

Inca soldiers

The Incas fought hard to defeat rival tribes and bring new lands under their control. Their army was well trained and highly organized, and was often led into battle by the emperor himself.

When a soldier killed an enemy, he sometimes made his victim's teeth into a necklace, to show what a brave warrior he was!

DEADLY SLINGS

At the beginning of a battle, the Inca soldiers used slings to hurl stones at

their enemies. These slings were made from plaited wool.

Inca soldiers wore thick cotton tunics and carried small wooden shields for protection. They had helmets made out of wood or cane to cover their heads.

Mountain roads

The Incas built a great network of roads to link all the parts of their huge empire together.

In the mountains, the roads zigzagged up and down the steep slopes, and rope bridges were built across deep ravines. The Incas had not discovered the wheel, so they did not have carts or chariots. All travel was on foot, and goods were transported on the backs of llamas.

Inca nobles were too important to walk. They rode in litters, carried by their servants'.

13

Clever builders

The Incas were skilful builders. Sometimes they used wood, and other times they used mud bricks – it all depended on what was available.

The most famous Inca buildings are the ones they made from stone. Using only simple tools, they shaped huge blocks so that they fitted together perfectly. Inca architects had no paper for drawing out their plans. Instead, they made small clay models for the builders to copy.

Inca workmen lifted blocks of stone into place to finish the side of a building at Machu Picchu, high up in the Andes mountains.

SHAPING STONES

Inca masons shaped the stones with tools made from bronze or stone. The stone blocks were then polished with sand.

Mountain farms

Most of the people that lived in the empire were farmers. Up in the mountains, the valleys were narrow and steep. The farmers cut steps, or terraces, to make the fields level enough for them to grow their crops. Fruit and vegetables were grown on the

Potatoes

Chilli peppers

Beans

Maize

INCA CROPS

These are some of the main crops that were grown by the Inca farmers.

warm, lower steps, maize was grown
on the middle terraces, and potatoes
were planted up on the higher,
colder levels. The farmers
grazed their llamas on
the high mountain
grasslands.

At home

Most Inca families lived in simple, one-roomed houses. They cooked food outdoors in clay pots, or sometimes on a clay oven indoors. The most usual meal was vegetable stew, made with potatoes and flavoured with hot chilli peppers. Only the wealthiest Incas could eat meat and fish regularly. Their favourite drink was chicha, a type of beer made from maize.

The Incas used clay to make beautiful pots for cooking and drinking. Some had carved or painted patterns, or pictures of people or animals.

AN INCA MODEL

To make this model, you will need $1\frac{1}{2}$ cups of flour, 1 cup of salt, $\frac{3}{4}$ cup of water, a pencil, a knife, and some poster paints.

1 Mix the flour and salt. Add the water gradually, until you have a soft dough.

2 Roll out the dough until it's about 2 cm thick.

3 Draw a llama shape, and cut it out with a knife.

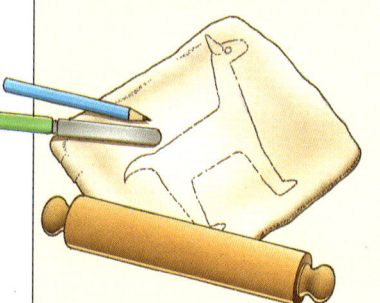

4 Bake at gas mark 2/ 170°C for 30 minutes. When the llama is cool, you can paint it.

Growing up

Most Inca children did not go to school. They worked with their families, herding llamas up in the hills, and spinning wool. Crafts such as spinning and weaving were passed on to children from their parents.

The sons of noblemen went to a special school in Cuzco. The boys studied the Inca language, Quechua, as well as religion, maths and history. Some students were also taught to 'read' the quipu.

THE QUIPU

The Incas did not use a system of writing, but used the quipu to keep records and to send messages. The quipu was made from many lengths of coloured, knotted string. Trained quipu readers were called quipucamayocs.

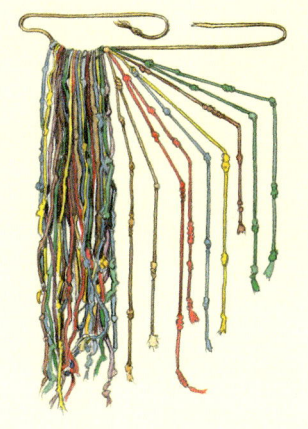

Music was important to the Incas. They played many instruments, such as these pan pipes.

Inca fashions

Inca clothes were made from cotton or wool, and were cut very simply. Men wore sleeveless, knee-length tunics, with a loin-cloth underneath. Women wore ankle-length dresses, with sashes tied around their waists. Over the top they might wear a cloak, which they fastened with a pin. They made their sandals out of leather, or plaited grass.

Men, women and children usually wore headbands. Some women also draped a veil over their heads and down their backs.

INCA GOLD

The Incas were skilled metalworkers. The emperor owned the gold and silver mines, as well as all the treasure that had once belonged to the people the Incas had conquered. The beautiful necklaces shown below were made from gold and turquoise.

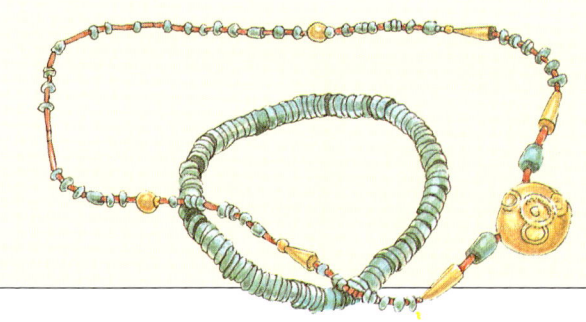

An Inca costume

Inca nobles wore finely woven tunics decorated with bright patterns, and heavy gold jewellery. Here's how to make your own Inca costume.

You will need an old sheet, some potatoes, card, newspaper, glue, scissors, a knife, and poster paints.

TUNIC

1 Cut the sheet into a rectangle, with a hole in the middle for your head. To stop the edges fraying, stitch a hem all round the tunic.

2 Cut the potatoes in half using a knife, and cut a simple shape from the cut surface.

3 Print the tunic by dipping the raised shape into thick paint, and pressing down firmly onto the cloth.

HEADDRESS

1 Cut a band of card to fit your head. Staple the band together.

2 Cut a jewel and a feather from card. Glue the jewel and feather onto the band, and paint it.

JEWELLERY

1 Draw the necklace shape and two ovals for the earrings onto the card, and cut them out. Make holes in each piece as shown. Paint the pieces with bright colours.

2 Thread the necklace with some string. Thread string through the earrings, and knot at the back, so that you can hook them over your ears.

Inca gods

Religion was an important part of Inca life. The chief god of the Incas was Viracocha, the Creator of all things. The Incas also worshipped the Sun god, Inti, and many others.

HOLY BEER

Beer in golden beakers was offered to the gods.

The Incas held important religious festivals at the beginning of each growing season, as they believed that the gods were responsible for the success or failure of their crops. After all the feasting, singing and dancing was finished, the hard work of planting the seeds would begin.

Mummies

When an emperor died, his corpse was turned into a mummy. This was done by drying out the body, and bandaging it in layers of cloth. The mummy was then dressed in fine clothes, and a beautiful golden mask was placed over its face. The mummy was kept in the palace, where it was guarded by servants.

During festivals, the mummies were carried through the streets in a great procession.

MAKE A MUMMY'S MASK

For this mask, you will need some thin card, scissors, paints, and elastic.

1 Draw the mask and the nose piece onto the card. Cut out the nose piece, and fold it up as shown below. Cut out the mask from the card.

2 Cut out holes for the eyes and nose, and glue the nose piece in position. Paint the mask, and make a small hole at either side.

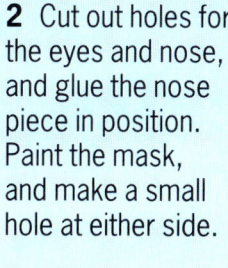

3 Thread elastic through the holes at the sides of the mask, adjust to fit around your head, and knot the ends.

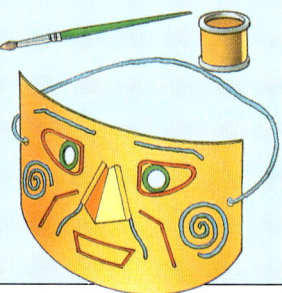

Index